■ DRUGS
The Straight Facts

Peyote and Mescaline

DRUGS The Straight Facts

■ DRUGS
The Straight Facts

Peyote and Mescaline

M. Foster Olive, Ph.D.

Consulting Editor

David J. Triggle

University Professor
School of Pharmacy and Pharmaceutical Sciences
State University of New York at Buffalo

CHELSEA HOUSE
PUBLISHERS
An imprint of Infobase Publishing

Peyote and Mescaline

Chelsea House
An imprint of Infobase Publishing
132 West 31st Street
New York NY 10001

Library of Congress Cataloging-in-Publication Data
Olive, M. Foster.
  Peyote and mescaline / M. Foster Olive.
    p. cm. — (Drugs, the straight facts)
  Includes bibliographical references and index.
  ISBN 0-7910-8545-7 (hardcover)
  1. Peyote—Juvenile literature. 2. Mescaline—Juvenile literature.
I. Title. II. Series.
  RS165.P44045 2007
  615'.7883—dc22   2006024075

Chelsea House books are available at special discounts when purchased in bulk quantities for businesses, associations, institutions, or sales promotions. Please call our Special Sales Department in New York at (212) 967-8800 or (800) 322-8755.

You can find Chelsea House on the World Wide Web at http://www.chelseahouse.com

Text and cover design by Terry Mallon and Keith Trego

Printed in the United States of America

Bang EJB 10 9 8 7 6 5 4 3 2 1

This book is printed on acid-free paper.

All links and Web addresses were checked and verified to be correct at the time of publication. Because of the dynamic nature of the Web, some addresses and links may have changed since publication and may no longer be valid.

Table of Contents

The Use and Abuse of Drugs

The issues associated with drug use and abuse in contemporary society are vexing subjects, fraught with political agendas and ideals that often obscure essential information that teens need to know to have intelligent discussions about how to best deal with the problems associated with drug use and abuse. *Drugs: The Straight Facts* aims to provide this essential information through straightforward explanations of how an individual drug or group of drugs works in both therapeutic and non-therapeutic conditions; with historical information about the use and abuse of specific drugs with discussion of drug policies in the United States; and with an ample list of further reading.

From the start, the series uses the word "drug" to describe psychoactive substances that are used for medicinal or non-medicinal purposes. Included in this broad category are sub-stances that are legal or illegal. It is worth noting that humans have used many of these substances for hundreds, if not thou-sands of years. For example, traces of marijuana and cocaine have been found in Egyptian mummies; the use of peyote and Amanita fungi has long been a component of religious cere-monies worldwide; and alcohol production and consumption have been an integral part of many human cultures' social and religious ceremonies. One can speculate about why early human societies used such drugs, but very likely it was for the same reasons we do—namely, to relieve pain and to heal wounds. Perhaps, anything that could give people a break from the poor conditions and the fatigue associated with hard work was considered a welcome tonic. Life in premodern cultures was likely to be, in the memorable words of 17th-century Eng-lish philosopher Thomas Hobbes, "poor, nasty, brutish, and short." One can also speculate about modern human societies' continued use and abuse of drugs. Whatever the reasons, the consequences of sustained drug use are not insignificant—addiction, unwanted side effects, overdose, and, for illegal, nonprescription drugs, incarceration, and drug wars—and must be dealt with by an informed citizenry.

The problem that faces our society today is how to break the connection between our demand for drugs and the willingness of largely outside countries to supply this highly profitable trade. This is the same problem we have faced since narcotics and cocaine were outlawed by the Harrison Narcotic Act of 1914, and we have yet to defeat it despite current expenditures in excess of approximately $20 billion per year on "the war on drugs" and the incarceration of a significant fraction of our citizens, particularly of minorities. The first step in meeting any challenge is to become informed about the nature of the challenge. The purpose of this series is to educate our readers so that they can make informed decisions about issues related to drugs and drug abuse.

SUGGESTED ADDITIONAL READING

Courtwright, David T. *Forces of Habit, Drugs and the Making of the Modern World*. Cambridge, Mass.: Harvard University Press, 2001. David T. Courtwright is professor of history at the University of North Florida.

Davenport-Hines, Richard. *The Pursuit of Oblivion: A Global History of Narcotics*. New York: Norton, 2002. The author is a professional historian and a member of the Royal Historical Society.

Huxley, Aldous. *Brave New World*. New York: Harper & Row, 1932. Huxley's book, written in 1932, paints a picture of a cloned society devoted only to the pursuit of happiness.

David J. Triggle, Ph.D.
University Professor
School of Pharmacy and Pharmaceutical Sciences
State University of New York at Buffalo

1

Hallucinogens: An Overview

A *hallucination* is something that we hear, see, smell, feel, or taste that does not really exist. Seeing a refrigerator change into a polar bear and begin walking around the room, or feeling as if your arms and legs have turned into tree limbs, are examples of hallucinations. Hallucinations are commonly experienced by people who suffer from mental disorders such as schizophrenia. Some people with schizophrenia hear voices telling them to do things, when in fact the voices are not real. These hallucinations are often frightening and disturbing.

Some people, however, find hallucinations enjoyable and stimulating—even life-changing spiritual or mystical experiences. They may take mind-altering substances collectively known as *hallucinogens* or *hallucinogenic* or *psychedelic* drugs. Hallucinogens are powerful chemical substances that produce hallucinations of all types. Commonly used hallucinogens include lysergic acid diethylamide (LSD), phencyclidine (PCP), magic mushrooms, and peyote. These drugs were very popular in the 1960s and 1970s, and their use continues today.

Some hallucinogens, such as LSD, PCP, or ketamine, are purely synthetic chemicals. Many other hallucinogens are derived from plants. Examples of these include the substances psilocybin and psilocin (which are found in certain types of wild [or "magic"] mushrooms); substances derived from plants found in South America, including dimethyltryptamine (DMT), 5-methoxy-dimethyltryptamine

(5-MeO-DMT), alpha-methyltryptamine (AMT), and 5-methoxy-N, N-diisopropyltryptamine (5-MeO-DIPT; commonly called "Foxy Methoxy" or "Foxy"); and mescaline, which is derived from the peyote cactus found in the southwestern United States and northern Mexico.

GENERAL PSYCHOLOGICAL EFFECTS OF HALLUCINOGENS

Different hallucinogens have different chemical structures, potency, and duration of psychological effects. LSD is the most potent, with less than a milligram needed to produce its effects. A typical LSD experience lasts 6 to 12 hours. It usually takes more than 10 milligrams (mg) of psilocybin, PCP, or ketamine to produce any effects, and the effects of these hallucinogens typically last a few hours. Mescaline is the least potent hallucinogen, requiring about 200 mg to produce any psychological effects, but it lasts the longest (usually 12 hours or more). On the other hand, the psychological effects of DMT last only for an hour or less, which is why this drug is said to offer a "businessman's trip." DMT is often smoked, so its onset of action occurs within seconds. Other hallucinogens, usually taken orally and then absorbed through the lining of the stomach or intestines before entering the bloodstream and ultimately the brain, take 30 to 90 minutes to kick in.

Despite their differing chemistries, all hallucinogens tend to produce roughly similar psychological effects. In general, hallucinogens produce a sense of time slowing down. Colors, touch, or sound may seem more intense. A person may feel as if his body is not his own. Shapes and objects may appear to change or "morph." The person may give increased attention to geometrical patterns and experience a sense of enlightenment and euphoria (a feeling of extreme pleasure and well-being). One common effect involves the "crossing over" of certain types of perception, such as "seeing" sounds or "hearing" colors. This type of experience is called *synesthesia*. Hallucinogens are often taken to increase one's self-awareness, and some users believe that they can communicate with God or other higher powers while under the influence of these drugs. The experience on a hallucinogen can vary from person to person, and is often dependent on one's personality and expectations about the drug, one's previous experience with it, and the social setting in which the drug is taken.

Physical effects that are commonly produced by hallucinogens, particularly mescaline and psilocybin, include dilation of the pupils, dizziness, nausea, vomiting, and increase in heart

TIMOTHY LEARY

One of the most famous users and advocates of hallucinogens was a man named Timothy Leary. Leary was a clinical psychologist at Harvard University who happened upon an article published in *Life* magazine in 1957 describing the psychological and mind-altering effects of "magic mushrooms." Leary was so intrigued by this article that he tried some of these mushrooms himself, and found it to be a life-altering experience. He felt as if hallucinogenic drugs were a good way to "free" one's psyche, learn more about one's self, and obtain a better understanding of life and the universe. Leary went on to found the Harvard Psychedelic Drug Research Program, where he gave hallucinogenic mushrooms to many graduate students and his fellow colleagues at Harvard, as well as some well-known artists, writers, and musicians. Leary also began to experiment with LSD. His work became increasingly controversial, though, because of academic and government policies opposing drug use, and Leary was dismissed from Harvard in 1963. He continued advocating the use of hallucinogens on his own (despite frequent brushes with the law), became the leader of the psychedelic movement of the 1960s and 1970s, and was often referred to as the "Galileo of Consciousness." He died in 1996.

rate, blood pressure, and body temperature. The intensity of these effects is dependent on dosage and an individual's biological makeup. The effects can be caused by the active hallucinogenic chemical itself, or impurities found within the drug.

DANGEROUS EFFECTS OF HALLUCINOGENS

Hallucinogens are not considered highly addictive in the same sense that drugs such as cocaine, methamphetamine, heroin, nicotine, or alcohol are. People rarely become physically dependent on hallucinogens; they don't experience withdrawal

Figure 1.1 *Timothy Leary, early pioneer and advocate of using hallucinogens, in a picture taken in 1968. © AP Images*

symptoms after stopping their use. They rarely go on hallucinogen binges, taking them in large amounts over a period of several days. There are some dangers, however, associated with using hallucinogenic drugs.

Sometimes users will experience a "bad trip," which can include intense fear and anxiety that lasts for hours. Why this happens is not known, but it is likely a result of an interaction between the drug, an individual's personality, and the environment in which the drug is taken. The following is an example of someone having a negative experience while on LSD:

> As I walked through the shopping mall, I noticed there were many people there, and all of them seemed to be looking at me. This made me feel uneasy, so I focused my eyes on the ground to avoid eye contact with anyone. As I turned the corner toward the food court, I couldn't resist looking up again to see if all eyes were still upon me. I did, but there were no eyes upon me. In fact, there were no eyes at all. Everyone's eyeballs were missing—in their place were empty holes in their skulls. I even passed by two twin girls being pushed in a double baby stroller by their eyeless parents, and as I looked down at the children's faces, even their eyes were missing. I felt a wave of fear and panic come over me. I could not bear the sight of these eyeless people, so I thrust my gaze downward and tried to focus on the pavement again. But somehow, in my state of extreme fear, I began to wonder if even my own eyes were still in their proper place. I found a storefront with tinted windows that provided a good reflection. As I stood about two feet from the glass, I gazed into my own eyes, and was horrified to see that my eyes were also missing from their sockets. Amazingly, I didn't even question the paradox that I could still see despite not having any eyes. I just turned and ran screaming in the direction of a nearby park. I must have blacked out,

because the next thing I remember is waking up at dusk in a grove of oak trees. The effects of the drug had worn off by then, but to this day, I still get the creeps every time I look in the mirror at my own eyes.

Bad trips can result in flashbacks, or sudden recurrences of images or memories of a negative experience while under the influence of the hallucinogen. These flashbacks can occur weeks, months, or years after the drug is used and are sometimes persistent. Occasionally, use of hallucinogens such as LSD can result in a complete psychotic breakdown that lasts for days or weeks. This state is characterized by a loss of touch with reality and mental problems such as delusions (false beliefs) and paranoia. Although these breakdowns are rare, they usually occur in people with preexisting psychiatric disorders, such as schizophrenia.

TRENDS IN HALLUCINOGEN USE

While the popularity of hallucinogens such as LSD and PCP exploded in the 1960s and 1970s, soon after their discovery, their use has been remarkably stable over the past several decades (see Figure 1.2). The use of DMT as a hallucinogen is a relatively recent occurrence, so there is little data on how many people use it on a regular basis. In the years 2000 and 2001, however, there was a dramatic spike in the number of people using a substance called 3,4-methylenedioxymethamphetamine (MDMA), also known as "ecstasy." Ecstasy is a derivative of methamphetamine that produces intense feelings of love and euphoria. It also produces enhancements in the perception of colors, sounds, and music, and for this reason it is sometimes classified as a hallucinogen. Since 2001, levels of ecstasy use have tapered off slightly, but the drug remains significantly more popular than LSD or PCP.[1]

Peyote and mescaline are used primarily by Native Americans in religious rituals. As a result, trends in their usage are not

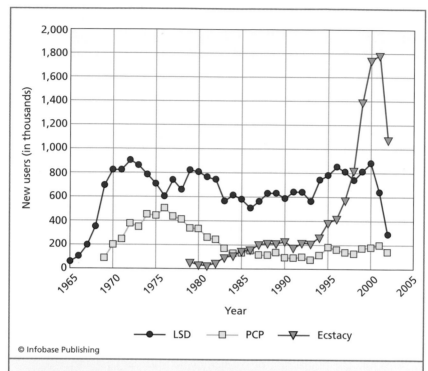

Figure 1.2 Number of new users of ecstasy, LSD or PCP in the years 1965–2003. Source: SAMHSA, Office of Applied Studies, National Survey on Drug Use and Health, 2002 and 2003

well documented in government studies. Yet, as can be seen in Figure 1.3, of all commonly used hallucinogens, teenagers try mescaline the least often. Perhaps this is because it is used mostly on Native American reservations and is relatively difficult to obtain by middle and high school students. LSD and ecstasy are the most often tried hallucinogens in this age group.

HOW HALLUCINOGENS WORK IN THE BRAIN

In the brain, *neurons* (nerve cells) carry electrical signals along wire-like nerve fibers called *axons*. At the end of each axon is a mushroom-shaped nerve ending called a *synaptic terminal*.

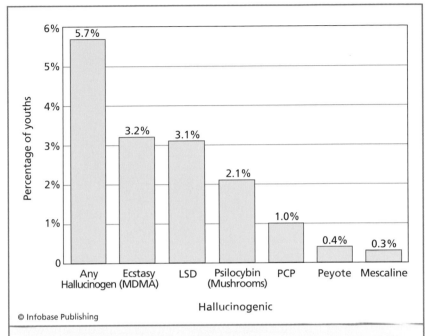

Figure 1.3 Data from the year 2001 showing the percentage of youths ages 12–17 who have tried a hallucinogen in their lifetime. Source: SAMHSA, Office of Applied Studies, National Survey on Drug Use and Health, 2002 and 2003

Axons can range from less than one millimeter to up to several centimeters in length. When the electrical signal traveling down the axon reaches the synaptic terminal, it causes chemical messengers called *neurotransmitters* to be released and secreted onto nearby neurons. This junction between a synaptic terminal and a nearby neuron is called a *synapse* (there are billions of synapses in the brain, and each neuron can have as many as 10,000 different synapses on it). After neurotransmitters are released, they diffuse away from the synaptic terminal into the synapse and encounter proteins called *receptors* on the surface of nearby neurons. Receptors are specific proteins that are designed to recognize specific neurotransmitters. When activated by neurotransmitters, these receptors can cause the

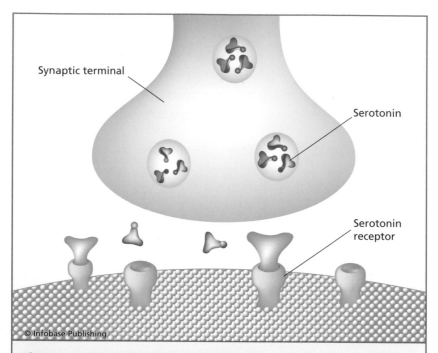

Figure 1.4 One of the main neurotransmitters in the brain is called sero-tonin, and a diagram of a serotonin-containing neuron is provided above. Keep in mind, however, that there are dozens of types of neurotransmitters that nerve cells can secrete. Other common neurotransmitters include dopamine, glutamate, gamma aminobutyric acid (GABA), noradrenaline, endorphins, and so on. Source: National Institute on Drug Abuse

nerve cell on which they reside to either become activated (so it passes along the electrical signal) or inhibited (so it doesn't pass the signal along).

Mescaline, LSD, and DMT produce their effects on the brain by mimicking the actions of serotonin, and thus altering how neurons communicate with each other. More specifically, these hallucinogens stimulate a subclass of serotonin receptors called 5-HT$_2$ receptors. PCP and ketamine act by inhibiting the func-tion of the N-methyl-D-aspartate (NMDA) receptor, which is normally stimulated by the neurotransmitter glutamate. Scien-tists are unsure precisely why either stimulating 5-HT$_2$ receptors

WHERE DO HALLUCINOGENS ACT IN THE BRAIN?

The brain has numerous regions that are each specialized for particular functions. So the effect a particular drug has on a person's thinking or behavior may depend partly on which brain region it is acting in. A diagram of basic brain structures and their functions is presented below.

Given that hallucinogens primarily affect perception, it is thought that they primarily act in regions of the brain such as the sensory cortex and visual cortex. They are also thought to act on a region of the brain involved in the perception of sound, known as the auditory cortex. Finally, since hallucinogens increase one's thoughts about religion, one's purpose in life, self-awareness, etc., it is believed that they also act in the frontal cortex, where a great deal of cognition occurs.

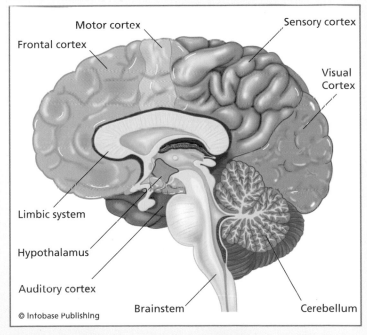

Figure 1.5 *Different brain regions have different functions.*

or inhibiting the function of NMDA receptors results in halluci-nations, but it likely has to do with how these receptors regulate the functions of neurons located in regions of the brain that control sensation, perception, and cognition (thinking).

2

What are Peyote and Mescaline?

Dry whiskey, divine cactus, divine herb, medicine of God,
flesh of God, devil's root, diabolical root, Indian dope,
dumpling cactus, turnip cactus, cactus pudding,
white mule, moon, "P," challote, the bad seed,
tuna de tierra (Spanish for "earth cactus").

These are some of the nicknames given to the peyote cactus (scientific name *Lophophora williamsii*), a spineless cactus plant that grows in desert regions of the southwestern United States and northern Mexico. The peyote cactus is often round-shaped and speckled with numerous little "bumps," "crowns," or "crests." (The scientific name *Lophophora* is derived from two separate Greek words meaning, "I bear crest.") These bumps can be cut off, dried in the sun into little discs (called "buttons"), usually between 1 and 4 inches in diameter, and eaten to give the user an intense psychological experience and hallucinations. Peyote cacti can also be adorned with light red or white flowers. Peyote cacti are very slow growing, taking up to 30 years from seedling to blooming of flowers.

The peyote cactus grows wild in certain regions near the Rio Grande River, which divides the United States from Mexico. The cactus is found mostly near the river in portions of Texas and northeastern Mexico (see Figure 2.3). In some areas, up to 60,000 peyote cacti can be located in a single acre of land.

Figure 2.1 Peyote cactus. © Francois Gohier/Photo Researchers

Plants that are consumed for their psychological effects contain many different chemicals. It is usually just a few of these chemicals, however, that produce the mind-altering effects. Tobacco and marijuana smoke, for example, contain several thousand different chemicals each, but it is only one substance (nicotine for tobacco, delta-9-tetrahydrocannabinol, or THC, for marijuana) that is thought to be the main psychoactive ingredient. The same is true for the peyote cactus. Of

Figure 2.2 Peyote buttons. © George Post/Photo Researchers, Inc.

all the chemicals found in peyote, the chemical *mescaline* is primarily responsible for the hallucinogenic properties of this plant. And still, there are more than 50 other potentially bioactive substances that may also contribute to the effects of peyote.

While the terms *peyote* and *mescaline* are often used interchangeably, even in this book, *peyote* refers specifically to the peyote cactus while *mescaline* refers to the main hallucinogenic chemical found in the peyote cactus. Also, *mescaline* should not be confused with *mescal* (or *mescale*), the name of both a tequila-like liquor and a toxic hallucinogenic bean grown in Texas. Neither the liquor nor the bean contains the psychedelic chemical mescaline.

Although possessing, selling, or smuggling the drug peyote is generally illegal in the United States, growing or cultivating the peyote cactus is not.

Figure 2.3 Map of the regions of the United States and Mexico where most wild peyote cactus plants are found.

OVERVIEW OF EFFECTS OF PEYOTE AND MESCALINE ON THE MIND

Mescaline (which belongs to a family of chemicals called "phenethylamines," pronounced "fen-eth-el-ay-meens") is chemically similar to other illegal drugs such as amphetamine and MDMA (ecstasy). Hallucinations induced by peyote and mescaline can range from mild to intense and typically last 6 to 12 hours. People who have taken mescaline report that the drug can produce a dreamy, almost delirium-like state with visual hallucinations. Users may see oddly shaped people or

OTHER CACTI AND PLANTS THAT CONTAIN THE PSYCHEDELIC CHEMICAL MESCALINE

The peyote cactus is not the only plant that contains mescaline. There are actually numerous plants (mostly cacti) that contain this chemical. Some examples of other mescaline-containing plants include *Lophophora diffusa, Trichocereus pachanoi* (also called the "San Pedro cactus"), *and Trichocereus peruvianus* (also called the "Peruvian Torch").

Even though *Lophora diffusa* and *Trichocereus* cacti contain mescaline, they don't necessarily produce the same psychedelic effects as peyote. This is because *Lophora diffusa* and the *Trichocereus* cacti contain additional psychoactive chemicals that can alter the effects mescaline has on the brain, producing different psychological effects.

Another cactus that contains mescaline is referred to by Native Americans as *peyotillo*, or "little peyote." This cactus (scientific name *Pelcyphora aselliformis*) is smaller than regular peyote cactus plants and does not contain as much mescaline. Native Americans use it for medicinal purposes.

While peyote is primarily found in the southwestern United States and regions of Mexico, *Trichocereus* plants are often found in the Andes Mountains of Peru in South America. Artifacts depicting peyote use and fossils of peyote plants have been found in various regions of the world dating back to approximately 8500 B.C. It is unknown, however, at what point in time people started using these cactus plants for their psychedelic properties.

creatures floating in the air, or buildings made out of strange things like bones or other body parts. Objects often appear to change shape or appearance rapidly. The user often feels like an alien in entirely new surroundings, and may feel as if he or she is floating or weighted down by some strange gravitational force. Light and colors are greatly intensified, and other sensations can be distorted (e.g., "seeing" sounds or "hearing" colors). Time is often perceived as passing more slowly. Often users experience intense feelings of love and understanding. It is common for them to believe they are communicating with God or other deities, and able to transcend the limits of earth, time, and space. It is for this reason that mescaline is often used during religious ceremonies, particularly by Native Americans, and that peyote is called the "divine" or "sacred" cactus.

Peyote and mescaline can also produce auditory hallucinations—hearing things in an altered way (often slowed down, with distorted pitch) or hearing sounds that are not really there. Some users report having conversations with objects, such as trees. Mescaline can also enhance the sense of smell. Hunger is often suppressed by peyote and mescaline, so reports of altered taste are not well documented.

The following passages are examples of the distorted thought patterns experienced by people who take mescaline:

> "The telephone pole and I chatted for quite a while. He has been around for only a few years, but has seen a lot of change in the city block where he resides. He is a happy pole, much happier than some of the older ones in the urban neighborhoods. He is particularly fond of the buses that stop at the bus stop a few yards away. He has made friends with several of them, and thinks that I would enjoy them as friends as well. I think he is right. I embraced the telephone pole as we said our goodbyes, and I hope to return someday to talk with my new-found friend."

"I watched the music pour out of the speakers from my stereo as if the music itself were some sort of fluorescent plasma. In faster parts of the music, the plasma flows like a raging river, but in the slower parts it is like a slow trickle. As the plasma hits the walls and ceiling, it bounces off, oftentimes splattering into an infinite number of plasma droplets that go off in all directions. When the lyrics begin, I can see the words in 3D block letters jumping out of the plasma river. The singer's voice is distorted and has a slight echo, but I can still make out the words. The guitar sounds like it is being played in a concrete cathedral, and the bass guitar causes everything in the room to appear blurry, almost as if it were vibrating very fast. Then come the drums...oh, the amazing drums. They sound extraordinarily clear and loud, but it doesn't hurt my ears. They pulse in my heart and my head, and I can feel my internal organs bouncing about inside me in rhythmic perfection. Time seems to have grinded to a halt. My CD player reads that we are a minute into the song, but it has felt like hours."

3

History of Peyote and Mescaline Use— Ancient and Modern

ANCIENT HISTORY OF PEYOTE AND MESCALINE USE

Only sparse details are known about the use of peyote and mescaline prior to the beginning of written history. Since peyote is grown mostly in what is now Mexico and the southwestern United States, it is believed that it was used primarily by local inhabitants of these regions for thousands of years before being introduced to people who lived elsewhere.

Archaeological evidence suggests that the peyote cactus has been around for at least 10,000 years. Fossils of the plant have been found in regions known to be inhabited by humans at the same time, and these fossils have been carbon dated back to approximately 8500 B.C. One recent group of archeologists and ethnobotanists found some fossilized peyote cactus in a cave near the Rio Grande in Texas, and carbon dated the fossil back to approximately 3700 B.C.[2] Amazingly, the mescaline chemical contained in the cactus was still intact. Other archaeological artifacts such as stone carvings and artwork that contain references to peyote have been found and dated back to several hundred years B.C. The fact that ancient peoples thought highly enough of peyote to adorn their artwork with it suggests that they may have known about its psychedelic properties.

Figure 3.1 Native American drawings, especially by those known to use peyote for religious purposes such as the Huichol tribe, often contained references to the peyote plant (notice the depiction of the peyote button in the center of the drawing). © Manu Sassoonian/Art Resource, NY

Soon after the Spanish explorer Hernán Cortés conquered the Aztecs of Mexico in 1519, the Spaniards learned of their use of peyote for medical and religious practices. When the Spaniards learned that this peculiar plant suppressed fear and hunger, they became worried that it might give their subjects enough courage to stage an uprising. So, by the year 1620, the Spaniards proclaimed that peyote was evil and the work of the devil. They likened the use of peyote to witchcraft and cannibalism. Its use was outlawed, with violations sometimes punishable by death.

Although the use of peyote was banned, some Native American tribes continued to use the cactus in secret. Two of these tribes, the Tarahumara and the Huichol tribe, are credited with carrying on the use of peyote into recent history.

MODERN HISTORY OF PEYOTE AND MESCALINE USE

By the 1800s, peyote use in Mexico had been forced underground. Peyote had also found its way back to Europe. The following is a brief timeline of the history of peyote and mescaline over the last 120 years:

1887— German scientist Dr. Louis Lewin receives a sample of dried peyote buttons. Not among his priorities, the container of peyote buttons is shelved for the next nine years.

1896— Dr. Lewin's colleague, Dr. Arthur Heffter, becomes interested in the chemical ingredients in the peyote buttons and isolates mescaline as the main psychedelic chemical. The chemical is named after the Mescalero Apache tribe of Native Americans, from whom the peyote buttons were obtained.

1918— The Native American Church (NAC), proponents of peyote use during religious ceremonies, is incorporated in Oklahoma City.

1919— Chemist Dr. Ernst Spath first synthesizes mescaline from raw chemicals in his laboratory.

1945— It is reported that mescaline is used in experiments on humans in Nazi concentration camps.

1947— U.S. Navy initiates its own set of experiments involving mescaline.

1952— A Canadian doctor named Humphrey Osmond begins examining the chemical similarities between mescaline and adrenaline (epinephrine) molecules.

1953— Popular novelist Aldous Huxley first experiments with mescaline under the supervision of Dr. Osmond, taking 400 mg of the drug.

1954— Huxley, enamored with the psychedelic effects of mescaline, publishes a book called *The Doors of Perception*, in which he recounts in detail his experiences with the drug. The book is later re-released in 1959, with new material discussing the notion that personal insight and spiritual revelation can be obtained through the use of hallucinogens such as peyote.

1970— The United States passes the Controlled Substances Act and classifies mescaline and peyote as Schedule I controlled substances, meaning that they have no medical value, are potentially addictive, and are not considered safe. The drug remains legal in Europe and may be purchased over the counter in various European countries.

1991— University of California at Berkeley professors Alexander Shuglin and his wife publish their famous book, *Phenethylamines I Have Known and Loved*, which documents their experimentation with over 250 hallucinogens, including ecstasy and mescaline.

1997— The U.S. military declares it will allow soldiers of Native American descent to use peyote for religious purposes. Approximately 0.5 percent of U.S. military service personnel are of Native American descent.

USE OF PEYOTE BY NATIVE AMERICANS

Of the many cultures and peoples throughout the world, Native Americans use peyote and mescaline the most. Not only

Figure 3.2 Aldous Huxley, author of *The Doors of Perception*, a book that detailed his experiences with peyote and mescaline. © AP Images

is the use of peyote ingrained in their culture and religion, but also any member of the Native American Church can actually use peyote legally under an exception in the Controlled Substances Act of 1970 (a discussion of this can be found later in this chapter).

In the seventeenth and eighteenth centuries, Spanish settlers exploring the more western parts of Mexico discovered

Figure 3.3 Navaho Indians, another American Indian group that includes peyote in religious ceremonies, holding all-night rites using peyote buttons in a hogan. © Time Life Pictures/ Getty Images

that peyote use was deeply embedded into the daily life of the isolated Native American tribes living there. These tribes included the Cora, Huichol, and Tepecana, who lived near the west coast of Mexico near what is now Guadalajara, and the Tarahumaras, who lived not too far from the Texas-Mexico border near the town that is now called Chihuahua.

The culture of the Huichol tribe was able to survive the suppressive influence of the Spanish. Anthropologists have described in great detail the tribe's use of peyote. In the Huichol religion, natural elements such as fire, air, earth, and water, are each considered a deity, and many other aspects of nature are thought to be divine. The Huichols believe that food is bestowed upon them by the gods, and that peyote (given to them by the gods) is useful for treating various diseases (also given to them by the gods). Huichol tribespeople make an annual pilgrimage to an area of Mexico called Wirikuta, also called "peyote land," where the peyote cactus is grown and harvested. The Huichols believe that a successful pilgrimage will ensure they receive adequate rainfall to grow their crops. This pilgrimage is approximately 300 miles, and before automobiles were invented, it used to take about 40 days to walk this distance. Once the Huichol pilgrims reach Wirikuta, a large religious ceremony and feast is held, and the peyote cacti are harvested and brought back to the Huichol homeland.

The Tarahumara tribe culture's emphasis on the importance of peyote also survived the anti-peyote sentiment of Spanish settlers. The Tarahumaras use peyote extensively for medicinal purposes and also engage in a pilgrimage to areas where peyote is grown.

INTRODUCTION OF PEYOTE INTO THE UNITED STATES

There is archaeological evidence that peyote was used by Native Americans as far back as 5000 B.C., in areas that are now in Texas near the Mexico-United States border. But, the introduction of peyote into the United States is credited to the Native American tribes of Mexico during the second half of the nineteenth century. It is believed that the tribes residing in the Gulf of Mexico and Rio Grande areas spread the use of peyote to the Kiowa, Comanche, and other Native American tribes that lived in what is now Oklahoma. From this region, the use of peyote in Native American culture and religion spread to other regions of the United States. The white, northern European settlers who ventured westward across the plains in the 1800s clashed with the Native Americans, though, and impeded the spread of peyote use. The whites generally viewed Native Americans as savages, and through violence and oppression eventually forced them from their homelands and onto reservations.

European settlers suppressed the beliefs, customs, and religious practices of Native Americans, even on their reservations. In an attempt to maintain some semblance of an independent culture, several religious movements were formed to promote Native American unification and inspire hope for the future. One of these religious movements was called *peyotism*. It was founded on the belief that the experience induced by peyote brought people to a higher spiritual state of enlightenment. The Indians believed that the European oppressors could not take this enlightenment away from them. Peyotism taught nonviolence, introspection (examining the self) and meditation, and acceptance of (or at least conciliation with) the European culture that had been forced upon Native Americans. Peyotism also focused on the healing powers of peyote. Many Native Americans accepted peyotism as their new religion, but it was not without opposition from European settlers as well as from some other Native American tribes. By the 1970s, most Native American tribes in the United States and Canada had been introduced to peyotism, thanks to evangelists, missionaries, and "prophets" who traveled the land in search of tribes to convert to the religion. Conversion of a tribe to peyotism was generally more successful if the tribal leaders were convinced to try the hallucinogen. The formation of the Native American Church aided in the spread of peyotism.

Like the Native Americans of Mexico, members of Native American tribes in the United States make pilgrimages to the land where peyote grows, although the religious rituals associated with this journey may differ from tribe to tribe. Today, peyote is still widely used by numerous Native American tribes throughout North America. Although primarily used during religious ceremonies and certain holidays or special events, some users take peyote regularly as an act of good faith or to promote physical and mental health.

THE NATIVE AMERICAN CHURCH

After the Europeans colonized North America during the fifteenth, sixteenth, and seventeenth centuries, most Native American cultures, languages, and religious practices were virtually wiped off the continent. As a result, many Native American tribes became disorganized, stricken with poverty and health problems, and fought battles with each other. In the late 1800s, Quanah Parker, a man of mixed Native American and European descent, led the Comanche tribe. When Parker became ill, he was taken to a "medicine man," who gave him peyote tea, which not only healed him but changed his whole outlook on life. Parker became an advocate of seeking peace and unity among all Native American tribes. He joined with a small group of Native Americans as well as some Europeans to form a religious organization called Peyote Road, which combined Native American and Christian values. Peyote Road taught compassion, nonviolence, independence, and self-reliance, and prohibited alcohol use, adultery, deceit and vengeance. It also advocated the use of peyote to battle medical ills and gain a clearer understanding of life's meaning.

In 1891, an anthropologist named James Mooney encountered the followers of Peyote Road. After spending time with its members, Mooney encouraged the group to establish itself as an official religious organization. The followers of Peyote Road were eventually incorporated as the Native American Church (NAC) in Oklahoma City in 1918. The members of this organization used peyote during religious ceremonies to broaden their spirituality and get to know and understand God. They even believed that peyote is the body of Christ, much the way Catholics believe that bread at communion is the body of Christ. As Comanche Chief Quanah Parker stated, "The white man goes into his church and talks about Christ; the Indian goes into his teepee and talks *to* Christ."

By 1922, the NAC had more than 13,000 members, and today its membership exceeds 300,000 within the United States and Canada. The NAC does not have recognized leaders, however, nor consistent rules for becoming a member or local chapter, or legally documented rituals. In addition, the NAC crosses tribal lines, and thus its members need not belong to one particular Native American tribe.

Figure 3.4 *Comanche Chief Quanah Parker. Source: Library of Congress*

WHAT IS A PEYOTE CEREMONY LIKE?

Religious ceremonies that include the use of peyote vary slightly from tribe to tribe and location to location, but in general have various common practices. The ceremonies are traditionally held at night and last for approximately 12 hours. Usually they are open to all ages and both males and females, although some tribes forbid women from participating. Prior to the ceremony, participants often make pilgrimages to the regions where peyote is grown to harvest the cactus plants. In some tribes, however, peyote is simply bought in bags of 1,000 dried buttons from local dealers called *peyoteros*. To enhance the psychedelic effects of the peyote, the participants usually fast for a day or so, so that the stomach absorbs the peyote more rapidly.

In a typical peyote ceremony, tribespeople gather at night and sit in a circle in a teepee around a fire and/or altar. They eat peyote buttons—as many as 30, depending on the size of the individual buttons—through the night. Sometimes the buttons are chewed slowly or crushed and made into a tea. Typically, there is singing, praying, chanting, drumming, and time for quiet reflection intermixed with the peyote consumption. Since peyote often produces nausea and vomiting, which is viewed by members as a way to cleanse and purify one's system, buckets or other receptacles are usually placed around the teepee. The prayers, songs, and quiet reflection, coupled with the effects of peyote, are intended to produce personal revelations. The participants feel that Peyote (also called the "High Spirit," which is a deification of the peyote cactus) "speaks" to them, promising forgiveness for sins and healing of physical illness.

After the ceremony, the participants usually engage in a large feast. They feel a great sense of unity and harmony. Often the tribal chief or host is thanked for leading the ceremony and providing an atmosphere of friendship and camaraderie.

CURRENT LEGAL STATUS OF PEYOTE
AND MESCALINE

The Comprehensive Drug Abuse Prevention and Control Act of 1970 (also called the Controlled Substances Act) made peyote and mescaline illegal by classifying them as Schedule I controlled substances. Schedule I substances are deemed to have no medical value (see Appendix 1 for further description of controlled substance classifications). This law, however, made the NAC exempt from its restrictions, allowing the use of peyote and mescaline for religious purposes. Specifically, the law allowed "use of peyote in bona fide religious ceremonies of the Native American Church."

There is controversy, though, over what exactly the NAC is. It is not centrally organized, and its leadership and membership are not well defined. Regulations regarding NAC membership vary from state to state; for example, Texas requires someone to be of at least 25 percent Native American heritage in order to participate in an NAC religious ceremony. Many other states may have no such restrictions (see Table 3.1). As a result, a person (Native American or not) can claim to be a member of the NAC and use peyote, asserting his or her right to exercise religious freedom. But there is no guarantee that a person's religious claim is sincere. The use of hallucinogens or other controlled substances during religious ceremonies remains an item of intense debate among state and federal lawmakers in the United States today.

In Texas, peyoteros must be registered with the state government and keep careful records of the quantities of peyote buttons they sell. As of 1996, there were approximately a dozen registered peyoteros in Texas. Each peyotero harvests and sells approximately 200,000 to 300,000 peyote buttons per year. Peyoteros often must seek permission or pay leasing fees to harvest peyote that is grown on private land.

According to the Controlled Substances Act, the punishment for possessing or selling peyote (or synthesizing mescaline

Table 3.1 Criteria for allowing use of peyote among the states with peyote laws.

State	Sincere religion intent	With a bona fide religious organization	Within an NAC ceremony	NAC membership required	Native American descent required	On reservations only	Incarcerated persons not exempt
AZ	X						
CO		X					
ID			X		X	X	
IA			X				
KS		X		X			X
MN		X					
NV		X					
NM		X					
OK			X				
OR	X						
SD			X				
TX				X	X		
WI			X				
WY				X			

Source: Boire, Richard Glen. "The Legal Root: State by state comparison of peyote statutes." The Entheogen Law Reporter vol. 1, no. 3. Available online at: http://www.peyote.net/archive/law.htm. Accessed on July 17, 2006.

with the intent to sell) is up to a $15,000 fine and/or five years in prison for the first offense. However, first offenders, if convicted, often get a more lenient punishment of one year's probation. The second offense is punishable by a fine of up to $30,000 and/or up to 10 years in prison. Only peyoteros and members of the NAC are exempt from this law.

Certain states have expanded the right to use peyote beyond what the federal government allows; for example, Arizona exempts from prosecution members of the Peyote Way Church of God and the Peyote Foundation in addition to members of the NAC. Minnesota exempts the American Indian Church, in addition to the NAC. Currently, there are 14 states with their own laws concerning peyote.

Native Americans assert their right to use peyote as part of their religious ceremonies under several laws, including the American Indian Religion Freedom Act of 1978, which bars the government from passing laws that "prohibit the use and possession of sacred objects necessary to the exercise of religious rites and ceremonies." Although this law did not mention peyote specifically, in 1994, the American Indian Religion Freedom Act Amendments were passed, which stated that, "for many Indian people, the traditional ceremonial use of the peyote cactus as a religious sacrament has for centuries been integral to a way of life, and significant in perpetuating Indian tribes and cultures." This act also states that, "the use, possession, or transportation of peyote by an Indian for bona fide traditional ceremonial purposes in connection with the practice of a traditional Indian religion is lawful, and shall not be prohibited by the United States or any State. No Indian shall be penalized or discriminated against on the basis of such use, possession of transportation..." Despite this freedom, the United States retained its right to impose "reasonable regulation and registration of those persons who cultivate, harvest or distribute peyote..." This is the reason that peyoteros must be registered with state governments, such as that of Texas.

For non-Native Americans, smuggling peyote or mescaline into or out of the United States is illegal. Since peyote buttons are relatively large, however, and the demand for them is relatively low, peyote trafficking is not currently a significant problem for the Drug Enforcement Administration.

In recent years, there has been a surge of lawsuits at the local, state, and federal government levels filed by people asserting that their religious freedom guarantees them the right

SALVIA–THE NEXT NEW HALLUCINOGEN?

Another recent legal battle has begun over a hallucinogenic plant called *Salvia divinorum*, which translated from Latin means "sage of the seers." Salvia (also known by such nicknames as Sally D, Magic Mint, Ska Maria Pastora, Shepherdess's Herb, and yerba de Maria) is a plant (part of the sage family of plants) that grows in the Sierra Mazatec region of Mexico. Like peyote, salvia has been cultivated and used by shamans ("medicine men," or tribal healers) for centuries, and its widespread use throughout Mexico is thought to have been suppressed by the Spanish Conquest. The use of salvia has gained popularity, particularly among young people, in recent years as a new legal way to have a psychedelic experience.

The leaves of the salvia plant contain a psychedelic chemical called salvinorin A. When eaten or smoked, the plant produces an intense dream-like state similar to other hallucinogens such as LSD or mescaline. First-time users, however, often find the experience produced by salvia to be unpleasant, or obtain no psychological effects at all. If smoked, the effects of salvia peak within a few minutes or so and last for up to 20 minutes; however, if salvia is eaten, the onset of effect is more delayed and the effects last for up to an hour or two, and the psychological effects may not be as intense as when it is smoked. The leaves of the salvia plant contain other psychoactive chemicals such as salvinorin B and G, divinatorin A, D and E, and salvincins A and B. The precise roles these other chemicals play in the psychological effects of salvia are not yet known.

Some of the effects of salvia are similar to those produced by mescaline. When Salvia reaches its peak effects, its users become easily distracted, less willing to socialize, have altered perceptions of color and time, may become fascinated with geometric patterns, feel as if they are floating, experience intense feelings of spirituality and understanding and feel as if they can communicate with higher powers, and may even experience full-blown hallucinations and out-of-body experiences. Also similar to mescaline, salvia users rarely report any type of hangover effect or addiction, but do sometimes have bad experiences and flashbacks. Unlike mescaline, psilocybin, and LSD, though, salvinorin A does not bind to serotonin receptors. Instead, salvinorin A binds to the same class of receptor protein that morphine and other opiate narcotics bind to.

Salvia is currently legal in most of the United States, and is sold in some tobacco shops as well as on the Internet. The Drug Enforcement Administration has salvia on its "watch list," though, and is considering making it a controlled substance. In addition, there have been several attempts by the U.S. Congress to classify it as a Schedule I controlled substance, but so far these attempts have failed. In the meantime, several states have placed their own restrictions on the salvia plant. In Louisiana, for example, it is illegal to sell *Salvia divinorum* if intended for human consumption, whereas it is still legal to own the plant. Missouri has classified salvia as a Schedule I controlled substance, and currently other states such as Illinois, New York, Alaska, and Delaware are considering similar classification. Salvia has been banned or restricted in several other countries including Australia, Belgium, Italy, and Sweden.

Figure 3.5 *A salvia dinorums or diviners sage. © Edward Kinsman/Photo Researchers, Inc.*

to use other illegal drugs, such as marijuana or some hallucinogens such as DMT. They claim that this right is protected
by the First Amendment of the Constitution and the Religious
Freedom Restoration Act of 1993, which states that the "government shall not substantially burden a person's exercise of
religion…" They argue that they should be allowed to consume any drug connected to their religion, even if it is an illegal drug.

Some of these religious groups have won victories in their
legal battles. The Uniao de Vegetal, for example, a Brazil-based
religious organization that uses ayahuasca (a tea containing the
hallucinogen DMT) in its religious ceremonies, had several
bottles of this tea seized by U.S. Customs officials at the organization's office in Santa Fe, New Mexico. The U.S. government
never filed criminal charges against the organization, but also
never returned the seized ayahuasca. In August 2002, the U.S.
District Court for New Mexico ruled in favor of the Uniao de
Vegetal, and the U.S. Supreme Court further upheld this ruling
in February 2006. The seized ayahuasca, however, has yet to be
returned to the members of the religious sect.

4

The Chemistry and Pharmacology of Mescaline

THE CHEMICAL STRUCTURE OF MESCALINE

Mescaline is the key hallucinogenic substance found in peyote and several other psychedelic plants, including the *Trichocereus* family of cacti. Mescaline belongs to a class of chemicals called phenethylamines. "Ecstasy" (MDMA) is another drug that belongs to this class. The chemical name of mescaline is 3,4,5-trimethoxy-beta-phenethylamine, and its chemical structure resembles that of other illegal drugs such as amphetamine as well as the brain's own neurotransmitters epinephrine (adrenaline) and norepinephrine (noradrenaline) (see Figure 4.1).

Mescaline is not a very potent drug, as it takes approximately 200 to 500 mg of the chemical to produce any psychedelic effects. Compare this with the less than 1 mg of LSD it takes to produce psychedelic effects. Mescaline has about 1/2000th the potency of LSD and about 1/20th the potency of psilocybin, the main psychoactive chemical in "magic mushrooms." A peyote button contains only approximately 45 mg (or less) of mescaline (only about 1 to 3 percent of its actual dry weight), and so it is necessary to ingest 4 to 12 peyote buttons to have any type of psychological effect.

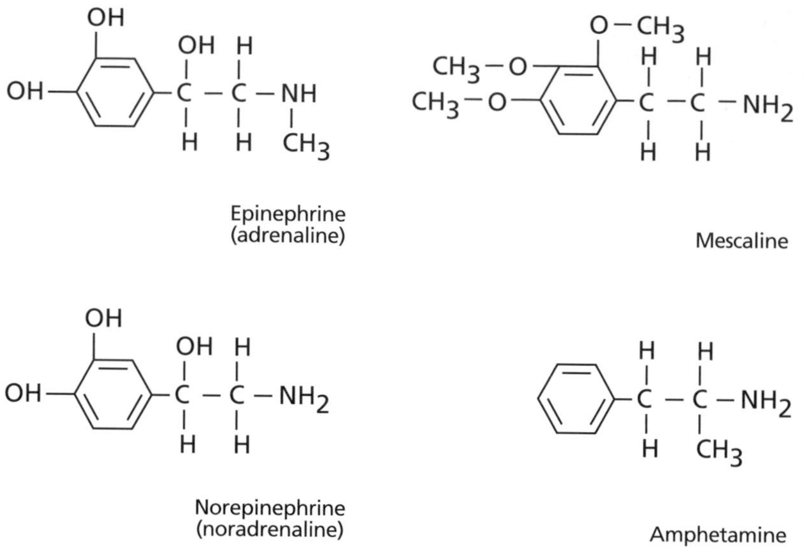

Figure 4.1 Chemical structure of mescaline. Note its resemblance to amphetamine and the neurotransmitters epinephrine (adrenaline) and norepinephrine (noradrenaline).

DURATION AND PHYSICAL EFFECTS OF MESCALINE

Depending on the amount taken, mescaline's psychedelic effects can last up to 12 hours, and they usually don't start until a few hours after ingestion of the peyote buttons. This is because mescaline has to be absorbed through the lining of the stomach before it enters the bloodstream and then the brain. (Other, more addictive drugs, such as cocaine or heroin, are smoked, snorted, or injected intravenously, allowing them to reach the bloodstream much more quickly). Factors such as the presence of food in the stomach and one's own metabolic rate can alter the onset and duration of the effects of mescaline.

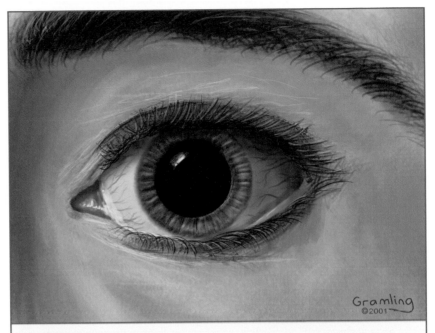

Figure 4.2 Illustration depicting a dilated eye. © Josh Gramling/ Phototake

In addition to its psychedelic effects, mescaline has numerous other effects on the body, including the following:

- increased heart rate and blood pressure

- increased patellar reflex of the knee

- dilation of the pupils

- increased perspiration

- increased motor activity and "fidgeting"

- changes in posture or difficulty walking

- changes in body temperature

- changes in levels of sugar, potassium, and white blood cells in the blood

- increased urination and salivation

- flushing (feeling hot) or chills

- nausea and vomiting (Peyote buttons have a very bitter and acidic taste, and ingesting the numerous buttons required to produce psychedelic effects often causes the user to feel nauseated and vomit.)

OTHER CHEMICALS FOUND IN PEYOTE

In addition to mescaline, the peyote button contains at least 55 other chemicals that are known to have active effects in the body. These chemicals can be classified as amino acids, alkaloids, or alkaloidal amines. It is thought that they contribute to the unique psychedelic effects that make the peyote experience different than one on pure mescaline. A complete list of these chemicals is given in Appendix 2. Examples of these chemicals include the following:

- *lophophorine*, a toxic substance that can cause convulsions; also causes a sickening feeling in the back of the head, facial flushing, a feeling of hotness (similar to that of a fever), and changes in heart rate

- *anhalodine*, a central nervous system stimulant

- *anhalonidine* and *pellotine*, central nervous system depressants that can cause drowsiness, apathy, lethargy, slowing of heart rate, drops in blood pressure, and, in large doses, paralysis

- *hordenine*, a cardiovascular stimulant that can also cause paralysis and respiratory arrest in high doses

- *dopamine*, one of the brain's natural neurotransmitters that is involved in motor control and feelings of pleasure

- *tyramine*, another substance found in the brain that is believed to play a role in how neurons communicate with each other

THE NEUROPHARMACOLOGY OF MESCALINE

One of the principal neurotransmitters in the brain is the chemical serotonin, also called 5-hydroxytryptamine (abbreviated 5-HT). Serotonin has many functions in the brain, including the control of mood, pleasure, hunger, sex drive, and sensation and perception. Over the years, scientists have discovered more than a dozen receptors for serotonin in the brain (recall that a receptor is a protein located on the surface of a nerve cell that binds a specific neurotransmitter and tells the neuron whether or not to change its electrical activity). These serotonin receptors are each encoded by a separate gene located on various chromosomes.

In the mid-1950s, soon after the discovery of LSD, scientists found that hallucinogens act by mimicking the actions of serotonin in the brain. It was later discovered that hallucinogens actually bind to and activate specific serotonin receptor types. For example, LSD activates numerous 5-HT receptor types, while mescaline appears to activate only the 5-HT_2 type of serotonin receptor.

So how does mescaline produce hallucinations? To date, neuroscientists are still not quite sure, but they are beginning to piece together the puzzle. It is believed that mescaline might produce hallucinations via its effects on a small region of the brain where sensory and perceptual information is processed. This region, located in the brainstem, is called the locus coeruleus (pronounced "LOW-cus ser-UHL-ee-us" and abbreviated LC), and it is packed with thousands of neurons that contain the neurotransmitter norepinephrine (also called noradrenaline). Neurons in the LC send long axons containing norephinephrine to many regions of the brain. The LC also receives input from many areas of the brain that are involved in sensation and perception of touch, taste, smell, sight, and sound. Scientists have discovered that the LC is packed full of 5-HT receptors and that neurons of the LC dramatically change their behavior when mescaline activates these receptors. The change in neuron behavior modifies how norepinephrine is released in many other regions of the brain. Thus, it is likely that mescaline stimulates serotonin receptors in the LC, which changes the ability of these neurons to respond normally to other input regarding sensation and perception. This, in turn, changes how norepinephrine is released in numerous other regions of the brain, which can then alter cognition and produce hallucinations.

Another region of the brain where mescaline is thought to act to produce hallucinations and changed thinking patterns is

MESCALINE, LSD, AND PSILOCYBIN— BIRDS OF A FEATHER?

Three of the most common hallucinogenic drugs used today are mescaline, LSD, and psilocybin. Some people insist that these three drugs produce the same psychological effects, and even some experienced users cannot tell the effects of each drug apart. Others, however, believe that the effects produced by psilocybin, LSD, or mescaline are unique. Several key pharmacological differences between these drugs are outlined in the table below:

	MESCALINE	LSD	PSILOCYBIN
Average dose	200–500 mg	0.05–0.2 mg	20–40 mg
Potency (relative to mescaline)	—	2000x stronger	20x stronger
Time to onset of effects	1–3 hours	30–40 minutes	20–30 minutes
Duration of effects	12+ hours	8–12 hours	4 hours
Occurrence of flashbacks	Rare	Common	Rare

the cerebral cortex. This region, which constitutes the bulk of our brain mass, is the highly wrinkled, outermost part of our brain (see Figure 1.4 in chapter 1), where thinking and planning are regulated. The cerebral cortex also processes sensory information coming from our eyes, ears, nose, mouth, and skin. As it turns out, the cerebral cortex is packed full of 5-HT$_2$ receptors, which are located on many neurons in this region. Scientists have found that stimulation of 5-HT$_2$ receptors in the cerebral cortex by mescaline causes these neurons to release their primary neurotransmitter, glutamate. In addition, the

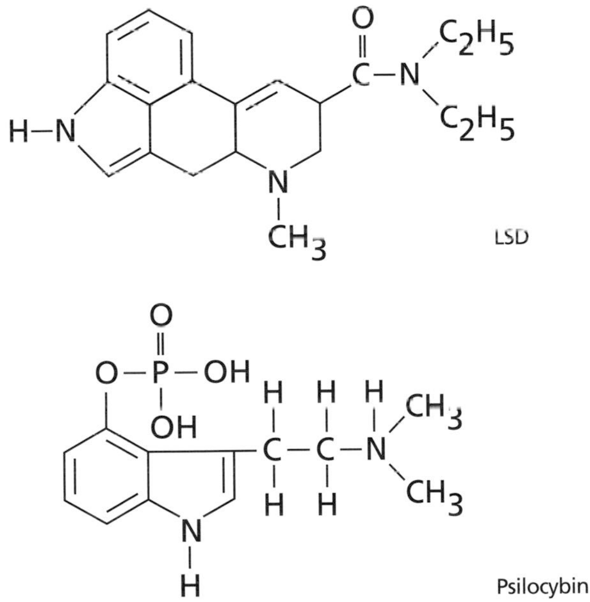

© Infobase Publishing

Figure 4.3 *Chemical structure of LSD and psilocybin*

changes in the activity of neurons in the LC, which release norepinephrine onto neurons in the cerebral cortex, also produce the release of glutamate in this region. This release of

MESCALINE KNOCKOFFS

Ken tried peyote several times, and while he enjoyed the psychedelic experience it gave him, he didn't like the nausea and vomiting it produced. Also, since Ken has a heart condition, he was worried that the cardiovascular effects of peyote might be bad for his heart. Ken had heard about some mescaline "knockoffs," or "copycat" psychedelic drugs, that some of his friends had tried. They were derivatives of mescaline and amphetamine and supposedly produced less nausea. So, Ken decided to give them a try. One drug he tried was 4-methyl-2,5-dimethoxyamphetamine (DOM), which was introduced into the California drug scene in the late 1960s and nicknamed "STP," for "serenity, tranquility, and peace." Ken liked it, but found it too sedating. One of Ken's friends then offered him a choice of a few other drugs that were new on the scene: 4-bromo-2,5-dimethoxyamphetamine (DOB), 4-bromo-2,5-dimethoxyphenethylamine (called "2C-B" or "Nexus"), paramethoxyamphetamine (PMA), and paramethoxymethamphetamine (PMMA). Ken's friend told him they were all similar to ecstasy, which Ken had tried previously and found to be a "good high." Ken tried PMMA, and it was the last drug he ever did. Shortly after taking it, he collapsed, went into cardiac arrest, and died. It turns out drugs such as PMMA are powerful amphetamine-like stimulants that cause the heart to race up to 160 beats per minute, and, particularly in people with heart conditions, can cause heart failure. Many of these drugs have killed users in both the United States and Europe. They are classified as Schedule I drugs by the Drug Enforcement Administration and are thus illegal to possess, sell, or consume.

glutamate likely causes disruption or hyperactivity of neurons of the cerebral cortex, resulting in the distortions in perception and logical thinking that are the trademark of hallucinogenic drugs. Similar disruptions in the activity of neurons in the cerebral cortex have been reported in people with schizophrenia. More research is needed to determine precisely how hallucinogens produce their effects on the brain and how this information might ultimately be used to treat people suffering from mental disorders characterized by hallucinations and disordered thinking, such as schizophrenia.

5

Psychological Effects of Peyote and Mescaline

Although some people, particularly Native Americans, use peyote and other mescaline-containing cacti for medicinal purposes, these plants are often ingested for the mind-altering psychedelic experiences they produce. Users may ingest the "divine cactus" in order to be taken to another world; to acquire new insights or knowledge about themselves, others, or their relationship with God; or to reduce inner conflict.

Comprehensive descriptions of peyote users' experiences (such as those in Aldous Huxley's book *The Doors of Perception*) are generally hard to come by. This is partly because people who use peyote find their experiences to be difficult to describe in words—they are too bizarre and disorienting. In addition, the visions and insights that people experience after taking peyote are often so deeply personal that they may be reluctant to share them with others.

Peyote experiences also vary considerably from person to person. Some may feel euphoric; others may feel lethargic; and still others may experience fright and panic. These individual differences are a result of the environment in which the drug is taken, and the personality, mood, attitudes, and beliefs of the user. Chemical factors, such as dosage or form of the mescaline (i.e., in peyote buttons, dried powder, or peyote juice or tea), also influence the experience. In general, pure mescaline produces generalized hallucinatory effects, whereas peyote buttons produce a more variable, complex, and unpredictable experience. This is likely because the peyote cactus contains many psychoactive chemicals besides mescaline.

Despite the wide variability in the type of experiences produced by peyote and mescaline, the effects usually occur in two different phases. During the first phase, beginning approximately 30 to 60 minutes following ingestion of the drug, some unpleasant physical effects start to take place, such as nausea, vomiting, stomach cramps, chills or hot flashes, trembling, headache, the need to urinate, chest pains, restlessness, and dilation of the pupils. As a result of this physical discomfort, some users may become anxious or depressed or become fearful that they are going to lose control over their bodies or die. This phase typically lasts for 30 to 60 minutes.

The second phase begins once the physical discomforts of the first phase dissipate, several hours after ingestion of peyote. The user begins to experience feelings of extreme pleasure, euphoria and elation, as well as dreamy sensory hallucinations. He or she may have "delusions of grandeur" (feelings of superhuman abilities), or become contemplative and introspective. Often the peyote user will also feel uncoordinated and have increased muscle reflexes during the second phase. This phase can last up to 12 hours.

Following are some of the most commonly reported experiences that occur during the second hallucinatory phase of peyote use:

DEPERSONALIZATION

"My legs were not my own. Even though they were attached to my body, they weren't mine. They surely belonged to someone else. But whose were they?"

A person experiencing "depersonalization," sometimes called "dual existence," does not feel like himself or herself.

Limbs may feel as if they are alien or have turned into tree branches, even though the person still retains control over them. Some peyote users also have "out-of-body" experiences—the sensation of looking at themselves from the outside. Some people experience these feelings of depersonalization as humorous or awe inspiring, while others may become frightened and panic.

DISORDERED THOUGHT PATTERNS

"The ceiling fan turned in a counterclockwise direction, then seemed to detach itself from the ceiling. In its place was a large hole, through which I found myself staring into a long spiral tunnel. The spirals also turned counterclockwise, and I became fixed on the pulsating white light at the far end of the tunnel. When I reached my hand out to try and touch the light, my hand detached from my body and turned to decaying flesh. I felt as if other parts of my body were also becoming detached. Would they ever come back, or were they lost forever?"

Often, a peyote user will experience a "furious procession" of thoughts and ideas. Before he or she has time to ponder a particular idea or image, another has come along and replaced it. Notice how in the preceding example the user cannot remain focused on a single item for very long.

ALTERED SENSE OF TIME AND SPACE

"As I sat and tried to write down my thoughts as they occurred, suddenly I felt as if I had been staring at these blank pages for hundreds of years. The table at which I was writing became very far away, and I was amazed I could even reach it."

The perception of time and space are often distorted by peyote. Some people feel that time slows to almost a standstill, while others feel that months or years have passed in the space of five minutes. Objects appear much closer or farther away than they actually are, and sometimes users

Figure 5.1 Perception distortions of space and time, not unlike those depicted in Salvador Dali's painting "The Persistence of Memory," are a common experience produced by mescaline.
© Bettmann/CORBIS; © Salvador Dali, Gala-Salvador Dali Foundation/Artists Rights Society (ARS), New York

have the sensation that they are looking the wrong way through a pair of binoculars. Hallways or tunnels may seem especially distorted.

COMMUNICATION DIFFICULTIES

"I was so entranced with the dancing trees that I didn't have a care in the world what was going on around me. My girlfriend kept asking me what I was seeing, but there was no way to describe it, and no time. I was afraid I would miss something if I started to talk. Besides, whatever I was currently looking at would be gone before I could get the first word out."

Perhaps because their minds are flooded with continuously morphing thoughts and images, or perhaps because the experiences they are having are too bizarre or complicated to describe in words, mescaline users often sit quietly without saying much to one another. They don't have much interest in communicating and would rather just sit and "enjoy the ride." Researchers who want people to relate their psychedelic experience to them while it is happening often become frustrated at their inability or lack of desire to communicate.

VISUAL AND PERCEPTUAL ALTERATIONS

Perhaps the most common (and desired) psychological effect of peyote and mescaline is the alteration in the perception of light, objects, sound, smell, or touch. Many people call these hallucinations "visions" and feel they are an extremely important part of the peyote experience. Some of the common visual and perceptual alterations that are experienced include the following:

- flashes of light occurring
- objects appearing to move rapidly or change size or shape
- the geometry of objects becoming intriguing
- objects appearing to have halos of light around them
- after-images or "trailers" appearing when objects move
- colors brightening and contrasts becoming enhanced
- images transforming into lattices, honeycombs, tunnels, alleys, or spirals

MEMORY LAPSES

"After I had come down [from the peyote high], I wanted to write down everything I had seen, heard, and felt. I started writing, but in the end I could only come up with a paragraph or two describing my experiences. I knew I had seen much more than that, but I just couldn't remember it all. My mind was too saturated."

While mescaline users are usually quite alert and awake during their psychedelic experience, afterward they often have

- the appearance of objects, animals, or people that are not really present, or the occurrence of vivid fantasies that are difficult to distinguish from reality
- "seeing" sounds, "hearing" colors

Figure 5.2 *Visual distortions caused by peyote and mescaline can include "trailers" like these captured in this photograph. © Alan Schein/zefa/Corbis*

difficulty recalling parts of it. Some researchers believe that these memory lapses occur because the mind becomes so flooded with thoughts and sensory perceptions that it is unable to filter and store all the information it is processing.

SPIRITUALITY

"Whether the clouds became God, or He became the clouds, I still do not understand. But as I recognized the unmistakable presence of the Almighty, I wanted to fall to my knees, but instead I felt as if He was lifting me up towards Him. I felt detached from the ground, but in His presence I did not care. I just wanted to speak with Him and find out why my baby brother had been taken from us, and if he was okay now that he was with the Father in heaven."

People who take peyote or mescaline often describe their experiences as very emotional and meaningful to

SYNESTHESIA

In the 1960s, novelist William Braden experimented with LSD and mescaline and wrote about his experiences in the book *The Private Sea.* (Although this book is mostly about LSD, it contains a postscript on Braden's experience with mescaline.) Braden tried mescaline while listening to a symphony by Beethoven, and as a result he began to "see" the music move about him in brilliant colors. Despite the extraordinary imagery and feelings that he experienced, Braden became so upset by the effects of mescaline that he asked that his experiment be terminated and that he receive an injection of the antipsychotic drug Thorazine. It took Braden several painful days to recover. Braden's experience, frightening to him as it was, is an example of what is called *synesthesia*, or a mixing of the senses. Braden's experience of sound turned into visual effects.

them, particularly if they believe they have communicated with God, Christ, or other higher powers. As a result, peyote or mescaline experiences often result in people having changed attitudes or beliefs, a greater understanding of themselves or others, or seeing their life in a different way in the grand scheme of the universe.

EMOTIONAL CHANGES

"The painting on my living room wall had been there for years, but I had never really noticed it. I mean, *really* noticed it. The colors and patterns were so fantastically integrated with the overall impressionistic theme that it could not have been painted by anyone less than a genius. And how supernatural it seemed that the raised texture of the oil paints were practically leaping off of the canvas, screaming to be admired. And I was truly their biggest admirer."

During a peyote experience, even minor events such as watching the sun set, seeing a shooting star, or even staring at one's own furniture or decorations can take on a tremendous emotional significance. As a result, peyote users often feel that their experience on the drug is mystical or life-changing.

LACK OF SEX DRIVE

"As my girlfriend and I dreamed the pleasant dreams of peyote, we felt a tremendous sense of love between us—like none we had ever experienced before. But neither of us had any interest in sex—it was not an option. It would have been a complete waste of time. There were too many better things to focus on."

Despite a heightened sense of perception, peyote users usually have little interest in sex; perhaps it is because their minds are too flooded with other thoughts and images. On a more biological level, the excess serotonin receptor activation on nerve cells resulting from peyote use also tends to reduce sex drive. Thus, the lack of interest in sex may be both bio-chemically and psychologically based.

ABSENCE OF DREAMS

Despite the vivid nature of the hallucinations and exaggerated sensory experiences produced by peyote, many users report that for several nights after having taken the drug, there is a general absence of normal dreaming during sleep. Perhaps the grandiose visions produced by peyote have actually replaced dreaming, albeit temporarily. More than likely, however, the stimulation of 5-HT$_2$ receptors by mescaline actually interferes with the normal cycles of various sleep stages intricately regulated by the brain.

6

Medicinal Uses
of Peyote

So far, we have discussed peyote and mescaline mostly in the context of their ability to produce intense psychedelic hallucinations. A vast majority of Native American peyote users, however, strongly believe that the peyote cactus and other mescaline-containing plants also have tremendous healing powers that can cure the ills of both the mind and the body. Many Native American cultures view illnesses as having supernatural causes (such as evil spirits), and believe that communication with higher powers through the use of peyote can help cure those illnesses. In fact, in many Native American dialects, the words for "medicine" are the same as those used for "peyote." (See Appendix 3 for a list of Native American words for peyote.)

Often there is no real distinction between medicine and religion in Native American cultures, and thus most "medicine men" in Native American tribes are also the tribe's spiritual leaders. Even when taken in religious ceremonies by Native Americans, peyote is used largely for its therapeutic properties. Many historians assert that the belief in the healing properties of peyote was largely responsible for the spread of peyote-based religions in the nineteenth and twentieth centuries. For example, Quanah Parker, a leader in the early establishment of the Peyote Road religion, became a believer in the healing powers of peyote when a Native American woman successfully treated him with the cactus, after he was severely wounded by a bull in Mexico. The purported healing powers of peyote were much more persuasive in converting others to its use than its ability to produce hallucinations.

Some Native Americans, particularly those in Mexico, use peyote preventatively to protect themselves from illnesses. They believe ingesting the cactus forms a barrier through which evil spirits cannot pass to inflict illnesses upon them. Other Native Americans, such as those in the United States, use peyote to cure diseases. They believe that peyote use, by allowing communication with supernatural powers as well as by causing vomiting, actually purges the mind and body of disease-causing evil spirits and toxins. In Peru, Native American healers, called *curanderos*, employ the mescaline-containing San Pedro cactus to fight the supernatural powers believed to cause disease. Not only do *curanderos* feed the cactus to the diseased patient to induce vomiting to purge the body of impurities, but the *curanderos* themselves also eat the cactus to enlighten themselves as to the nature of the patient's disease. Others believe that the vomiting produced by eating peyote is punishment for one's sins. Some Native American tribes believe peyote has health benefits only when taken as part of nightlong religious ceremonies, whereas other tribes believe peyote can be taken at any time for medicinal purposes.

Since peyote and mescaline are illegal for most U.S. citizens to possess or use, there has been little scientific study of the medicinal value of these substances. There are many diseases and illnesses (cancer, broken bones, blindness, headaches, viral infections, etc.) that users believe the peyote cactus can cure. In this chapter we will focus on just a few of them.

PEYOTE AS AN ANTIBIOTIC

It is widely believed by many Native Americans that peyote may be an effective treatment for various types of infections, and there has been research on whether peyote possesses antibiotic activity. In the 1960s, researchers at California State

University at Fullerton, studying bacteria growing in petri dishes, showed that peyote extracts were capable of killing various strains of the bacteria *Staphylococcus aureus* (which causes infections of the skin when bacteria enter an open wound). This same group of researchers showed that peyote could reduce infections in mice inoculated with toxic strains of this same bacteria.[3] Subsequent research showed that the ingredient of the peyote extract responsible for its antibiotic actions is *peyocactin,* later renamed *hordenine.* Attempts to replicate the results of these researchers have failed, but medical science has since created many antibiotics that are much more potent and effective than hordenine.

THE USE OF PEYOTE IN PSYCHOTHERAPY

The ability of peyote and its active ingredient mescaline to produce profound psychological effects—reducing conflicts a person may have within himself or with others, increasing the expression of emotions, producing a deeper understanding of life's meaning—has prompted many psychologists to ponder the potential benefits of using the drug as an aid in psychotherapy. Up until the 1970s, there were various published reports that peyote and mescaline helped patients identify, understand, and resolve their psychological problems, and was especially useful when all other medications or therapies had failed. There were as many published reports, however, showing that using peyote and mescaline as an aid in psychotherapy was not feasible, primarily because the drug produced a lack of ability (or willingness) on the part of the user to communicate. In addition, in some patients the visual imagery and hallucinations produced by peyote and mescaline were so terrifying that they had to be administered a tranquilizer to halt the effects of the drug. Some therapists feared that the bizarre hallucinations and confused thinking produced by mescaline might actually become more of a problem than the psychological disorders they were initially

PEYOTE'S EFFECTS AND THE SYMPTOMS OF SCHIZOPHRENIA

In the middle of the twentieth century, two physicians, Dr. Humphrey Osmond and John Smythies, recognized the similarities between the psychedelic effects of mescaline and the psychotic symptoms of the psychological disorder schizophrenia.[4] They noted that both mescaline and schizophrenia produce distortions of sensory perception, dissociated and random patterns of thinking, depersonalization, paranoia, hallucinations, and, at times, agitation and violence. Osmond and Smythies proposed that mescaline could be a way to "model" the psychosis of schizophrenia in order to study its causes and potential treatments.[4] This ability of peyote to mimic the symptoms of psychosis led to its being referred to as a "psychotomimetic" (i.e., psychotic- or psychosis-mimicking) drug.

Figure 6.1 *Dr. Humphrey Osmond, an early researcher of the similarities between the symptoms of schizophrenia and the effects of mescaline.* © Bettmann/Corbis

In the years that followed the publication of Osmond and Smythies' paper, however, it became evident that there are distinct differences between the psychedelic effects of mescaline and the symptoms of schizophrenia. First, the hallucinations produced by mescaline are primarily visual, whereas those in schizophrenia are primarily auditory (hearing voices is very common). Also, mescaline produces a state of disorganized thinking and distorted sensory perceptions that persist continuously for hours on end, whereas in schizophrenia, these symptoms come and go on a minute-by-minute or hour-by-hour basis. Thus most psychiatrists today believe that the usefulness of mescaline as a model for schizophrenia may be limited only to being a model of acute schizophrenia.

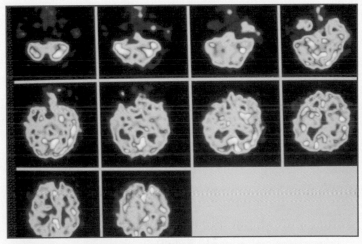

Figure 6.2 *A series of positron emission tomography (PET) scans of a schizophrenic patient's brain during hallucinations. They depict a range of activity from low (blue) to high (yellow) and illustrate a disruption of the brain's normal, roughly symmetrical patterns. © Tim Beddow/Photo Researchers, Inc.*

trying to treat. During the 1960s and 1970s, ecstasy (MDMA) and LSD became more available and popular to use as psychedelic drugs than mescaline or peyote. This, along with the U.S. government classifying mescaline as a Schedule I controlled substance in 1970, has caused the use of peyote and mescaline as aids in psychotherapy to virtually disappear.

CAN PEYOTE TREAT ALCOHOLISM?

Alcoholism affects all races and cultures, but it is particularly prevalent among Native American tribes. Some believe this to be a result of genetic factors; others blame it on the introduction of alcohol to Native Americans by European settlers; while still others blame it on the nature of Native American culture. Regardless of the cause, alcoholism is a serious health risk to any individual, as it can lead to liver problems and certain types of cancers, malnutrition, brain damage, and even death.

Members of the Native American Church regularly use peyote to treat people with alcoholism or other types of drug addiction. They recommend that it be taken every day for a few weeks or months, with hopes that the person will be cured of their addiction. Despite anecdotal reports that peyote can be used to cure someone of alcoholism, scientific research suggests that psychedelic drugs, when given in a hospital or laboratory setting, rarely produce any changes in motivation or attitude that might lead a person to give up drinking alcohol or taking drugs. Rather, it is thought that the combination of an influential tribal leader, a close-knit group of followers and supporters, and the deep self-awareness brought on by the peyote experience may lead a person to change his or her beliefs and attitudes toward substance abuse.[5] Thus, to anyone outside the Native American culture, peyote is probably of limited use in treating any type of addiction.

USE BY MEDICAL PROFESSIONALS IN THE WESTERN TRADITION

In the late 1800s, several physicians wrote about the possible medical uses of peyote in early medical journals; for example, Dr. S.F. Landry wrote about the beneficial effects of peyote on cardiac and respiratory ailments.[6] Drs. D.W. Prentiss and F. P. Morgan wrote that peyote was very useful in the treatment of muscle spasms and should also be used in the treatment of depression and epilepsy.[7,8] Then, in the early 1900s, peyote was listed in a major drug reference manual (then called the *United States Dispensatory*) as being potentially beneficial in the treatment of various medical illnesses. Around 1920, though, peyote was deleted from this book, and it has not been discussed as a potentially therapeutic agent in any major medical reference book since. Today, most doctors shun the idea of using any type of hallucinogenic drug for treatment of disease, believing that better therapies, with fewer psychological side effects, exist.

USE OF MESCALINE IN GOVERNMENT EXPERIMENTS

It has long been suspected, with some supporting evidence, that the governments of some countries of the world have experimented with hallucinogenic drugs on people. While many of these experiments involved LSD, there are some reports that mescaline was also used. In their book *Acid Dreams*, Martin Lee and Bruce Shalin recount some of the instances of human experimentation using mescaline and LSD. During World War II, for example, many prisoners of war were given hallucinogens in attempt by their Nazi captors to gain mind control and extract information. The Nazi military had spent many years searching for "truth serum" drugs that would make prisoners reveal secret information about military plans, whereabouts of troops and their leaders, and so on. In the 1940s, Nazi doctors at the concentration camp in Dachau,

Germany, gave mescaline to several dozen prisoners and found that while they could not impose their will on prisoners (as could be done under hypnosis), even after giving them very high doses of mescaline, they could get prisoners to reveal intimate secrets following discretely phrased questions.

The U.S. government was also engaged in a search for their own truth serum during World War II. Following the war, the Central Intelligence Agency (CIA), formerly known as the Office of Strategic Service (OSS), initiated Project CHATTER in 1947. This Project was an exploration of methods to obtain information from people without the use of torture. Dr. Charles Savage conducted mescaline experiments on both humans and animals for this Project at the Naval Medical Research Institute in Bethesda, Maryland. Ultimately U.S. scientists found mescaline to be an ineffective truth serum (as with many other tested drugs), and Project CHATTER was terminated in 1953.

Problems Associated with the Use of Peyote and Mescaline

Many people who use peyote or mescaline, especially those who have fought for its legalization and the right to use it in religious ceremonies, assert that the drug is safe. When compared to "harder" drugs such as crack cocaine, heroin, methamphetamine, and so on, the known ill effects of mescaline do appear less serious. Addiction to and physical dependence on mescaline is almost unheard of; however, as with any mind-altering chemical, there are some serious potential health problems associated with using peyote or mescaline.

DEATH

Death resulting from peyote or mescaline use is rare. It is difficult to overdose on peyote because it produces vomiting, which purges the body of excess levels of mescaline and the other chemicals found in the peyote cactus. The lethal dose of mescaline in humans is not known, but in monkeys it is 130 milligrams per kilogram (kg) of body weight.[9,10] Extrapolating to humans, this would mean that an average 70 kg (150 lbs) adult would have to ingest approximately 9 grams of mescaline (equivalent to over 200 peyote buttons) at one time for death to result. Fortunately, the vomiting induced by peyote usually prevents this from occurring.

Mescaline and peyote can cause complications, however, if used by people with preexisting health conditions. People who have liver or heart disease, for example, may have adverse reactions to mescaline or peyote, including liver failure or heart attack.

There are reports of people who have died after taking peyote or mescaline as a result of the hallucinations or disordered thinking they experienced; for example, in the 1980s, a man who had taken peyote died after jumping off the cliffs overlooking a beach in California. Presumably he thought he could fly.

TOLERANCE AND WITHDRAWAL

When a person takes peyote or mescaline, even for the first time, he or she usually develops tolerance to it, meaning that more of the drug is needed to produce the same effect. This tolerance lasts a few days, so if eight peyote buttons are taken on one night, it might take 10 or 12 buttons to produce the same effect a week or so later. Other psychedelic drugs such as LSD or psilocybin can produce "cross-tolerance": if someone takes LSD one night and peyote the next, higher amounts of peyote will likely be needed to achieve the same psychedelic effects.

Immediately following a peyote experience, the user tends to feel fatigued (perhaps because he or she stayed up all night). Some people have reported feeling anxiety or depression after the drug wears off. In fact, it is not uncommon for someone who has taken any psychoactive drug that makes them feel euphoria (be it mescaline, cocaine, amphetamine, ecstasy, or whatever) to subsequently feel depressed (the so-called crash). There are rarely any withdrawal symptoms if one discontinues taking the drug.

GASTROINTESTINAL PROBLEMS

Peyote is a bitter and foul-tasting substance containing many alkaloid substances that make the user prone to vomit. As a result, repeated usage of the drug can lead to gastrointestinal problems. Repeated vomiting can cause stomach acid to eat away at the mucus lining of the esophagus and mouth, causing ulcers, and can dissolve tooth enamel. (Similar problems are reported in people with bulimia, who also vomit frequently.) Abdominal pain and cramping from vomiting is also a side effect of repeated peyote use.

LONG-TERM PSYCHOLOGICAL EFFECTS

Repeated use of many psychoactive drugs is thought to cause damage to nerve cells in the brain, resulting in specific psychological or cognitive impairments; for example, repeated use of ecstasy, marijuana, or LSD has been linked to memory loss, emotional problems, and impulsivity. Since Native Americans take peyote many times a year, and often begin taking peyote during childhood as part of religious ceremonies, it raises the question of whether long-term use of this substance leads to any psychological problems. In a recent study addressing this, medical researchers from Harvard University surveyed members of the Navajo Nation, a religious organization within the Navajo tribe (which has over 250,000 members, more than a third of them members of the Native American Church).[11] These researchers studied 97 peyote users (either with or without a history of alcoholism), using a variety of psychological tools, including memory and vocabulary tests, cognitive ability tests, and intelligence tests. The test results were compared with those of a group of 79 Navajos without any history of major drug use (including peyote). The study showed no difference between the psychological performance of the long-term peyote-using Navajos and the non–drug-using Navajos. In fact, increased psychological problems were only found in the Navajos that had a history of alcoholism, who showed difficulties with memory tasks. This is consistent with numerous other studies showing evidence for diminished mental functions in alcoholics. This study was one of the first

Figure 7.1 "The Scream" painted by Edvard Munch hints at the sort of disturbing imagery or emotions one might feel during a bad trip. © Burstein Collection/CORBIS; © The Munch Museum/The Munch-Ellingsen Group

of its kind to examine the long-term effects of peyote, and was particularly reassuring to the U.S. military, since more than 10,000 of its service members are also members of the Native American Church and assert their right to use peyote as part of religious ceremonies.

BAD TRIPS AND PSYCHOTIC REACTIONS

While many people report that peyote and mescaline produce euphoria, others have reactions to the drug that are far from enjoyable. Some people have described their experiences with peyote and mescaline as "terrifying" and "horrific." This kind of reaction may be brought on by the physical effects of the drug (increased heart rate, sweating, nausea, vomiting), which sometimes create the sensation that the user is going to lose control or die. Others become so paranoid and suspicious that they may become violent toward those around them. Users can also develop delusions (false beliefs) and feel that other people or things are intent on harming them. This type of reaction is often referred to as a "psychosis," and resembles some of the symptoms of schizophrenia.

Most of the time the bad experience a person has with a hallucinogen is related to the vivid imagery and hallucinations it produces. As shown in the example on the following page, frightening images of monsters or scenes of gore or tragedy can be perceived as real.

HALLUCINOGEN PERSISTING PERCEPTION DISORDER

Sometimes weeks, months, or even years after taking a hallucinogenic drug such as mescaline, LSD, or psilocybin, some of the perceptions experienced can creep back into consciousness unexpectedly. Months after Jenny's bad experience (see box on following page), for example, when she would daydream in class and stare at the floor, the floor would seem to turn into lava as in her experience in Europe. This brought back terrible memories of the night she took peyote. Such flashbacks are the hallmark of Hallucinogen Persisting Perception Disorder, or HPPD, which is a psychological problem recognized by the American Psychiatric Association.

One of the key criteria for a diagnosis of HPPD is that flashbacks or visions occur when the person has not taken any

A VISIT TO HELL

Jenny was just 19 when she tried peyote while traveling in Europe with some of her college friends. They bought a bag of peyote buttons from someone on the street and decided to take the drug in the safety of their hotel room. The three of them dimmed the lights and sat in a circle on the floor. Two of Jenny's friends, Kelly and Amanda, got very sick and vomited after eating just two buttons, and decided not to continue. Jenny did not get so sick and within a few hours of eating eight peyote buttons, she started to experience some very bizarre visions and hallucinations. The floor of the hotel room turned to lava, and she began to feel hot and as if she was going to get burned, so she leaped up onto the bed. When she glanced out the hotel window, the lights coming in from outside appeared to turn red, and then it looked as if blood was splattered all over the window. Jenny then felt as if the bed mattress had disappeared from underneath her and that she was falling into a deep black hole. This falling sensation lasted for over an hour. When she felt like she hit the bottom, she began to try to climb out of this gigantic pit she found herself in. As she clawed at the walls, her fingers fell off of her hands, and when they hit the ground, they turned to snakes. As she screamed for help, she saw her words floating in the air and then disintegrating into flames. Jenny glanced up at the top of the pit and saw a huge demon looking down at her, sneering and floating downwards. The demon then lashed at her with his three-fingered talons, and she began to scream even louder. She felt pain in her entire body, although her body appeared to be not her own, and each of her five senses felt like they belonged to five different people. Jenny felt overwhelmingly helpless and like she was going to be tortured forever. Eventually, the demon faded into the walls of the pit, and the torture subsided. "This must be what hell is like," she thought.

drugs for weeks or months. In addition, the visions or distorted perceptions cannot be a result of any other medication, medical condition, or psychiatric disorder, such as schizophrenia. Finally, in order to meet the diagnosis for HPPD, it is essential that the flashbacks are upsetting and interfere with the person's functioning in his or her job, school, or family or social life.

The flashbacks typically resemble the hallucinations experienced under the influence of the drug—flashes of light, geometric shapes, halos, afterimages, objects changing texture or shape, or a distorted sense of space and time. The flashbacks can occur spontaneously or be triggered by stress, anxiety, fatigue, or entering into an environment similar to the one where the drug was originally taken. They often seem real for a short time but can eventually be distinguished from reality. Symptoms of HPPD usually disappear over the course of several months, but some people have reported that they can last five years or longer. The disorder can be treated with anti-anxiety drugs such as Valium or antidepressants such as Paxil or Zoloft. Psychotherapy may also help patients to cope with the persistent flashbacks as well as identify potential triggers.

HPPD is most commonly experienced after taking LSD, but can occur after taking any type of hallucinogenic drug, including mescaline. Research into this relatively rare disorder has shown it is likely a result of long-term changes in brain chemistry brought on by taking hallucinogenic drugs.

In his famous book, *The Doors of Perception*, Aldous Huxley stated that peyote has the potential to push one's mental state from sane to insane. He wrote that the peyote experience is "inexpressibly wonderful…to the point almost of being terrifying. And suddenly I had an inkling of what it must feel to be mad."

TREATMENTS FOR BAD TRIPS

Although panic and fear reactions are more likely to occur after taking LSD, they also can be experienced with mescaline or psilocybin. Before bad experiences were better understood, they were actually considered to be part of the normal psychedelic experience. In the 1960s, people taken to the emergency room during a bad trip would often have their stomach emptied (or "pumped") to rid the gastrointestinal tract of any remaining unabsorbed drug. This was futile, because most, if not all, of the drug would have already been absorbed into the bloodstream. Sometimes people suffering from a bad trip were diagnosed as psychotic and admitted to a psychiatric hospital.

As the medical profession began to recognize a bad trip as a common, adverse side effect of hallucinogenic drugs, hallucinogen users started seeking medical help and treatments became more effective. Today, people suffering from this effect are usually given a tranquilizer such as Valium to sedate them until the hallucinogen wears off.

SLEEP DISTURBANCES

Some peyote users report that they don't dream while sleeping during the first few nights after having taken peyote. But in some cases peyote's effect on sleep can be far more dramatic. Recently, a case was reported in which a man with a history of alcohol abuse as well as posttraumatic stress disorder (PTSD) became psychotic after taking part in a Native American peyote ritual.[12] The 54-year-old Native American man had drunk some peyote juice during a healing ceremony and later came to believe he was being hunted by animal spirits. As a result, he was unable to sleep for two weeks. He then began to experience visual and auditory hallucinations about those spirits. The man was so disturbed by his hallucinations that he became depressed and resorted to coaxing young children into performing religious rituals. His fellow tribespeople eventually persuaded him to go to a psychiatric hospital to seek relief for his symptoms. There, he was given the antidepressant medication trazodone and soon fell asleep for 15 straight hours. After awakening, the man's psychotic symptoms and hallucinations were completely gone.

It is unknown whether or not the man's psychotic symptoms were a direct result of the effects of peyote or of his prolonged sleep deprivation. His history of alcohol abuse and PTSD might have made him susceptible to the ability of peyote to produce symptoms of psychosis. It is remarkable that his symptoms completely disappeared after one episode of prolonged sleep, whereas most psychotic patients take days, weeks, or months of strong antipsychotic medications to have their symptoms reduced.

In summary, while many people assert that peyote and mescaline are safe and even potentially beneficial substances with little or no potential for addiction, there are some potential hazards associated with the use of these drugs that should not be overlooked. The most serious of these hazards is the potential for a negative experience or psychotic reaction, which can result in long-lasting psychological problems including flashbacks and Hallucinogen Persisting Perception Disorder. In rare cases the dissociation from reality caused by peyote has resulted in actions that can be harmful or fatal to the user or surrounding people.

Appendix 1

DRUG ENFORCEMENT ADMINISTRATION CLASSIFICATION OF CONTROLLED SUBSTANCES

In 1970, the U.S. government passed the Controlled Substances Act, which classified all drugs into one of five categories, or "schedules." In effect, this law classified drugs and other substances according to how medically useful, safe, and potentially addictive they are. These schedules are defined as follows:

Schedule I—The drug has (1) a high potential for abuse, (2) no currently accepted medical use in the United States, and (3) a lack of accepted safety. Peyote and mescaline are classified as a Schedule I substance, as are marijuana, heroin, ecstasy, psilocybin, LSD, DMT, and Foxy.

Schedule II —(1) The drug has a high potential for abuse, (2) the drug has a currently accepted medical use in the United States or a currently accepted medical use with severe restrictions, and (3) abuse of the drug may lead to severe psychological or physical dependence. Cocaine, morphine, methamphetamine, and d-amphetamine are examples of Schedule II substances.

Schedule III —(1) The drug has less potential for abuse than the drugs in schedules I and II, (2) the drug has a currently accepted medical use in treatment in the United States, and (3) abuse of the drug may lead to moderate or low physical dependence or high psychological dependence. Anabolic "body-building" steroids, ketamine, and many barbiturates are examples of Schedule III substances.

Schedule IV—(1) The drug has a low potential for abuse relative to the drugs in Schedule III, (2) the drug has a currently accepted medical use in treatment in the United States, and (3) abuse of the drug may lead to limited physical dependence or psychological dependence relative to the drugs or other substances in Schedule III. Anti-anxiety drugs such as Valium and Xanax, as well as prescription sleeping pills such as Ambien, Lunesta, Halcion, and Dalmane are examples of Schedule IV substances.

Schedule V—(1) The drug has a low potential for abuse relative to the drugs or other substances in Schedule IV, (2) the drug has a currently accepted medical use in treatment in the United States, and (3) abuse of the drug may lead to limited physical dependence or psychological dependence relative to the drugs or other substances in Schedule IV. Certain narcotic-containing prescription cough medicines such as Motofen, Lomotil, and Kapectolin PG are classified as Schedule V substances.

Controlled substances can be reclassified by the Drug Enforcement Agency (DEA) as newer data or evidence becomes available indicating medical usefulness or increased addiction potential. Peyote and mescaline, however, remain classified as Schedule I controlled substances, just as they were when the Controlled Substances Act was originally passed in 1970.

Appendix 2

LIST OF CHEMICALS FOUND IN THE PEYOTE CACTUS

Mescaline is the major hallucinogenic chemical found in the peyote cactus, but this cactus contains numerous additional chemicals that may also contribute to its psychedelic effects. For this reason, the effects of eating peyote buttons may be different than those experienced if one were to take pure synthetic mescaline. The following is an alphabetic list of these chemicals:

3,4-dihydroxy-5-methoxyphenethylamine

3,4-dimethoxyphenethylamine

3-hydroxy-4,5-methoxyphenethylamine (also called 3-demethylmescaline)

4-hydroxy-3-methoxyphenethylamine

anhalamine

anhalanine

anhalodine

anhalonidine

anhalotine

candicine

dopamine

epinine

hordenine

isoanhaladine

isoanhalamine

isoanhalonidine

isopellotine

lophophorine

lophotine

mescaline (3,4,5-trimethoxy-beta-phenethylamine)

mescaline citrimide

mescaline isocitrimide lactone

mescaline maleimide

mescaline malimide

mescaline succinimide

mescaloruvic acid

mescalotam

mescaloxylic acid

N,N-dimethyl-3-hydroxy-4,5-dimethoxyphenethylamine

N,N-dimethyl-4-hydroxy-3-methoxyphenethylamine

N-acetyl-3-hydroxy-4,5-dimethoxyphene-thylamine (also called
N-acetyl-3-demethylmescaline)

N-acetylanhalamine

N-acetylanhalonine

N-acetylmescaline

N-formyl-3-hydroxy-4,5-dimethoxyphene-thylamine (also called
N-formyl-3-demethylmescaline)

N-formylanahalamine

N-formylanhalanine

N-formylanhalonidine

N-formylanhalonine

N-formylmescaline

N-formyl-O-methylanhalonidine

N-methyl-3-hydroxy-4,5-dimethoxyphenethylamine

N-methyl-4-hydroxy-3-methoxyphenethylamine

N-methylmescaline

N-methyltyramine

O-methylpellotine

pellotine

peyoglunal

peyoglutam

peyonine

peyophorine

peyoruvic acid

peyotine

peyoxylic acid

S-(-)-anhalonine

S-(-)-lophophorine

S-(+)-O-methylanhalonidine

tyramine

Source: Anderson, E.F. *Peyote: The Divine Cactus*, 2d ed. Tucson, Ariz.: The University
of Arizona Press, 1996.

Appendix 3

NATIVE AMERICAN NAMES FOR PEYOTE

Various Native American tribes refer to peyote using the following common names. In many Native American languages, the term for peyote is often the same as that for medicine.

Tribe	Name for Peyote
Comanche	wokowi or wohoki
Cora	huatari
Delaware	biisung
Huichol	hicouri, hukuli, hicori, jicori, and xicori
Kickapoo	pee-yot
Kiowa	seni
Mescalero Apache	ho
Navajo	azee
Omaha	makan
Opata	pejori
Otomi	beyo
Taos	walena
Tarahumara	híkuli
Tepehuane	kamba or kamaba
Wichita	nezats
Winnebago	hunka

Source: Anderson, E.F. *Peyote: The Divine Cactus*, 2d ed. Tucson, Ariz.: The University of Arizona Press, 1996.

Notes

1. U.S. Government Printing Office (2002, 2003). National Survey on Drug Use and Health, Substance Abuse and Mental Health Services Administration, Office of Applied Studies, Washington, DC.
2. El-Seedi, H.R., P.A. Smet, O. Beck, G. Possnert, and J.G. Bruhn. "Prehistoric peyote use: alkaloid analysis and radiocarbon dating of archaeological specimens of *Lophophora* from Texas." *Journal of Ethnopharmacology* 101 (2005): 238–242.
3. McCleary, J.A., P.S. Sypherd, and D.L. Walkington. "Antibiotic activity of an extract of peyote (*Lophophora williamsii* [Lemaire] Coulter)." *Economic Botany* 14 (1960): 247–249.
4. Osmond, H., and J. Smythies, J. "Schizophrenia – a new approach." *Journal of Mental Science* 98 (1952): 309–315.
5. Pascarosa, P., S. Futterman, and M. Halsweig. "Observations of alcoholics in the peyote ritual: a pilot study." *Annals of the New York Academy of Sciences* 273 (1976): 518–524.
6. Landry, S.F. "Notes on Anhalonium lewinii, Embelia ribes and Cocillana." *Therapeutic Gazette* (3d serial) 5 (1889): 16.
7. Prentiss, D.W., and F.P. Morgan. "Anhalonium lewinii (mescal buttons)." *Therapeutic Gazette* (3d serial) 11 (1895): 577–585.
8. Prentiss, D.W., and F.P. Morgan. "Therapeutic uses of mescal buttons (Anhalonium lewinii)." *Therapeutic Gazette* (3d serial) 12 (1896): 4–7.
9. Speck, L.B. "Toxicity and effects of increasing doses of mescaline." *Journal of Pharmacology and Experimental Therapeutics* 119 (1957): 78–84.
10. Hardman, H.F., C.O. Haavik, and M.H. Seevers. "Relationship of the structure of mescaline and seven analogs to toxicity and behavior in five species of laboratory animals." *Toxicology and Applied Pharmacology* 25 (1973): 299–309.
11. Halpern, J.H., A.R. Sherwood, J.I. Hudson, D. Yurgelun-Todd, and H.G. Pope Jr. "Psychological and cognitive effects of long-term peyote use among Native Americans." *Biological Psychiatry* 58 (2005): 624–631.
12. Lu, B.Y., C. Woofter, and R. Escalona. "A case of prolonged peyote-induced psychosis resolved by sleep." *Journal of Clinical Psychiatry* 65 (2005): 1433–1434.

Bibliography

General

Anderson, E.F. *Peyote: The Divine Cactus*, 2d ed. Tuscon, Ariz.: The University of Arizona Press, 1996.

Gahlinger, P.M. *Illegal Drugs: A Complete Guide to their History, Chemistry, Use and Abuse*. Las Vegas, Nev.: Sagebrush Press, 2001.

Chapter 1

Grinspoon, L., and J.B. Bakalar. *Psychedelic Drugs Reconsidered*. New York: The Lindesmith Center, 1997.

Nichols, D.E. "Hallucinogens." *Pharmacology and Therapeutics* 101 (2004): 131–181.

Chapter 2

Grinspoon, L., and J.B. Bakalar. *Psychedelic Drugs Reconsidered*. New York: The Lindesmith Center, 1997.

Chapter 3

Leonard, I. "Peyote and the Mexican inquisition." *American Anthropologist* 44 (1942): 324–326.

Chapter 4

Halpern, J.H. "Hallucinogens and dissociative agents naturally growing in the United States." *Pharmacology and Therapeutics* 102 (2004): 131–138.

Aghajanian, G.K., and G.J. Marek. "Serotonin and hallucinogens." *Neuropsychopharmacology* 21 (Supplement 2, 1999): 16S–23S.

Chapter 5

Braden, W. *The Private Sea*. Chicago: Quadrangle Books, 1967.

Grinspoon, L., and J.B. Bakalar, *Psychedelic Drugs Reconsidered*. New York: The Lindesmith Center, 1997.

Hermle, L., M. Funfgeld, G. Oepen, H. Botsch, D. Borchardt, E. Gouzoulis, R.A. Fehrenbach, and M. Spitzer. "Mescaline-induced psychopathological, neuropsychological, and neurometabolic effects in normal subjects: experimental psychosis as a tool for psychiatric research." *Biological Psychiatry* 32 (1992): 976–991.

Chapter 6

Lee, M.A., and B. Shalin. *Acid Dreams: The Complete Social History of LSD: The CIA, the Sixties, and Beyond*. New York: Grove Press, 1986.

Chapter 7

American Psychiatric Association. *Diagnostic and Statistical Manual for Mental Disorders,* 4th ed. Washington, DC: American Psychiatric Press, 1994.

Halpern, J.H., and H.G. Pope. "Do hallucinogens cause residual neuropsychological toxicity?" *Drug and Alcohol Dependence* 53 (1999): 247–256.

Halpern, J.H., and H.G. Pope. "Hallucinogen persisting perception disorder: What do we know after 50 years?" *Drug and Alcohol Dependence* 69 (2003): 109–119.

Huxley, A. *The Doors of Perception: Heaven and Hell.* Harmondsworth, UK: Penguin Books, 1959.

Reynolds, P.C., and E.J. Jindrich. "A mescaline associated fatality." *Journal of Analytical Toxicology* 9 (1985): 183–184.

Further Reading

Aberle, D.F. *The Peyote Religion Among the Navaho,* 1st ed. Chicago, Ill.: Aldine Publishing Company, 1966.

Anderson, E.F. *Peyote: The Divine Cactus,* 2d ed. Tucson, Ariz.: The University of Arizona Press, 1996.

Calabrese, J.D. "Spiritual healing and human development in the Native American Church: Toward a cultural psychiatry of peyote." *Psychoanalytical Review* (1997) 84: 237–255.

Gahlinger, P.M. *Illegal Drugs: A Complete Guide to their History, Chemistry, Use and Abuse.* Las Vegas, Nev.: Sagebrush Press, 2001.

La Barre, W. *The Peyote Cult,* 5th ed. Tulsa, Okla.: University of Oklahoma Press, 1989.

Stewart, O. *Peyote Religion: A History,* 1st ed. Tulsa, Okla.: University of Oklahoma Press, 1987.

Web Sites

Drug Addiction.com
Hallucinogens, disassociative drugs, and their effects.
http://www.drug-addiction.com/hallucinogens.htm

Drug Enforcement Administration
History and facts about hallucinogens.
http://www.usdoj.gov/dea/pubs/abuse/8-hallu.htm

Drug Enforcement Administration—Office of Diversion Control
List of Schedule 1 controlled substances.
http://www.deadiversion.usdoj.gov/schedules/listby_sched/sched1.htm

Free Vibe.com
Drug facts, personal stories, links to resources, and more.
http://www.freevibe.com/

Partnership for a Drug-Free America
Brief review of peyote (includes photographs).
http://www.drugfree.org/Portal/drug_guide/Peyote#

Index

Index

Index

About the Author

M. Foster Olive received his bachelor's degree in psychology from the University of California at San Diego, and went on to receive his Ph.D. in neuroscience from UCLA. He is currently an assistant professor in the Center for Drug and Alcohol Programs and Department of Psychiatry and Behavioral Sciences at the Medical University of South Carolina. His research focuses on the neurobiology of addiction, and he has published in numerous academic journals including *Psychopharmacology* and *The Journal of Neuroscience.*

About the Editor

David J. Triggle is a University Professor and a Distinguished Professor in the School of Pharmacy and Pharmaceutical Sciences at the State University of New York at Buffalo. He studied in the United Kingdom and earned his B.Sc. degree in Chemistry from the University of Southampton and a Ph.D. degree in Chemistry at the University of Hull. Following post-doctoral work at the University of Ottawa in Canada and the University of London in the United Kingdom, he assumed a position at the School of Pharmacy at Buffalo. He served as Chairman of the Department of Biochemical Pharmacology from 1971 to 1985 and as Dean of the School of Pharmacy from 1985 to 1995. From 1995 to 2001 he served as the Dean of the Graduate School, and as the University Provost from 2000 to 2001. He is the author of several books dealing with the chemical pharmacology of the autonomic nervous system and drug-receptor interactions, some 400 scientific publications, and has delivered more than 1,000 lectures worldwide on his research.